Psalm Journal
Book II

Joan Chittister, O.S.B.
Mary Lou Kownacki, O.S.B.

Sheed & Ward

Copyright © 1985 by
Joan Chittister, OSB

All rights reserved. No part of this book may be reproduced or transmitted in any form or by any means, electronic or mechanical, including photocopying, recording or by an information storage and retrieval system without permission in writing from the Publisher.

Sheed and Ward™ is a service of National Catholic Reporter Publishing, Inc.

ISBN: 0-934134-45-6

Published by: Sheed and Ward
P.O. Box 40292
Kansas City, MO 64141

Contents

A Psalm Journal: What It Is and How to Use It v

Week Twenty-Seven, Psalm 18	1
Week Twenty-Eight, Psalm 77	5
Week Twenty-Nine, Psalm 49	9
Week Thirty, Psalm 92	13
Week Thirty-One, Psalm 46	17
Week Thirty-Two, Psalm 19	21
Week Thirty-Three, Psalm 36	25
Week Thirty-Four, Psalm 59	29
Week Thirty-Five, Psalm 63	33
Week Thirty-Six, Psalm 38	37
Week Thirty-Seven, Psalm 122	41
Week Thirty-Eight, Psalm 21	45
Week Thirty-Nine, Psalm 26	49
Week Forty, Psalm 30	53
Week Forty-One, Psalm 32	57
Week Forty-Two, Psalm 35	61
Week Forty-Three, Psalm 51	65
Week Forty-Four, Psalm 61	69
Week Forty-Five, Psalm 71	73
Week Forty-Six, Psalm 94	77
Week Forty-Seven, Psalm 144	81
Week Forty-Eight, Psalm 90	85
Week Forty-Nine, Psalm 92	89
Week Fifty, Psalm 84	93
Week Fifty-One, Psalm 89	97
Week Fifty-Two, Psalm 119	101

A Psalm Journal:
What It Is and How to Use It

Let me tell you about this simple little book. It comes out of the prayer life of a living community. It links ancient insight and present circumstances, prayer and personal growth. It will enable you to compare your own reflections to the faith-sharing of others. It will fill your mind and heart with the deepest themes of the Judeo-Christian tradition. And, by the time you have completed it, you yourself will have written half the book.

In monastic communities, the Liturgy of the Hours — psalms, canticles and readings from Scripture — are the basic prayer of the day. Every morning and evening of every day of their lives, the Benedictine community gathers to celebrate the presence of God in time, to proclaim their hope in the morning and their faith in the night, to engage in the dialogue of the spiritual life that the meditative listening to the scriptures intends. As the years pass then, these psalms of praise and pain, of success and defeat, shape a contemplative vision that sees the will and face of God in every event, in every human cry from the beginning of time until now. It was in those moments of daily community prayer and personal reflection that this Psalm Journal began.

As prioress of the community, I began to shape reflections and the blessings that end every period of public prayer from the insights that the psalms of the day had raised in me. Then, in accord with the oldest of monastic traditions, I encouraged the community to memorize the verse or two on which my reflections were based. Finally, I suggested that those phrases become the basis for the community's own contemplative centering that day as they went from distraction to distraction, from task to task, from meeting to meeting, too pressed to allow themselves long periods of daily private prayer or reading. Now I'm urging you to do the same thing.

Eastern religious practice depends heavily on the choice and repetition of *mantras*. The *mantra* is a word or saying whose meaning is simple enough to call us to the real center of life and faith when everything around us threatens to draw us away. It's not a theological tract; it's not liturgical practice; it's not even a long prayer formula. It is a brief recall of the great truth of life.

The psalms, I suggest, are the Judeo-Christian *mantras*. Sung for centuries, they have captured the spiritual reality of one generation after another. They sing of praise and fear and faith and final victory. They sing all the human emotions to God. They talk to God. They scour the world for answers. They ring across time in the human memory.

And when sight is dim and hearing diminished, these verses that we hold in memory may well be all we have left of the universal answers to the great questions of life.

How to Use This Book

This book invites you to memorize the psalm part, to consider the personal reflections and literary variations that follow each and then to write from your own experience what these words mean to you. In that way, this little book will become your own faith journal. You'll see what ideas form the basis of your faith life, what events have brought you to growth, which bother you, which challenge you to think more deeply, which occur again and again, which life insights are just coming to consciousness in you.

The process is divided into five parts. You can complete them in one reflection period or you can divide each reflection into five parts or days. It works like this:

Day One. Simply memorize the verse. Say it over and over. Come back to it many times during the day. Let it sink into the rhythm of your walk or breathe with it as you look out the window for a minute or recall it at the beginning of each hour or make it the quiet beginning of everything you do. Say it to yourself before you start the car, or open the meeting, or begin the dishes. Use it over and over and over until the verse is automatic, until it comes without effort.

Day Two. Read the first reflection. Say the psalm verse to yourself thoughtfully several times. Now, read the first reflection, mine, and write out the answer to the question it asks or make a written comment on the reflection itself. Do you understand it or not? What in it has the most meaning for you and why? What problem does it present? What questions does it raise? The important thing is that, as on Day One, you continue to repeat it to yourself over and over throughout the day.

Day Three. Read the second reflection. After having considered what the psalm verse had said to me, Sister Mary Lou tested these insights from the psalms against other ancient wisdom or figures from contemporary literature. Then she wrote a question of her own about it.

So now, say the versicle to yourself thoughtfully several times and then read the story or quotation that extends the psalm idea. Again, write down your answer to the question that follows it or the feelings and faith-questions that this passage raised in you. Repeat the verse prayerfully throughout the day.

Day Four. Write your own reflection. Real prayer is not a discipline; it is a relationship with God. The psalms mean different things to different people, depending on what is going on in their own lives at that time. Say the psalm verse to yourself thoughtfully several times. Now think: What thoughts or problems or insights into your own life has it raised in you? Write all of that out as diary, or dialogue with God, or testimony, or debate. Write as much or as little as you want, but write. With feeling and with honesty. Say the psalm verse over and over throughout the day.

Day Five. The psalm lives in me. Write the psalm verse from memory in the space provided. Say it aloud if you can. Involve every sense in the owning of this insight. Then, complete the sentence, "At this point in my life, this psalm verse . . ." Think, in other words, what the insights you've gained in the course of these reflections demand from you in a specific way and in this specific moment or period of your life. How and when will you carry out the action suggestion? Contemplation, remember, is not for its own sake. Contemplation changes life.

Your *Psalm Journal* is the beginning of contemplation. It is the link between the spiritual and the active dimensions of life. Most of all, it is the start of a rich, quiet life of growth in interior prayer that brings peace and faith and reflection and wisdom to the clatter and chaos that is so much a part of modern life.

I encourage you to do the *Psalm Journal* with someone else: with a friend, with a prayer group, with your husband or wife. Sharing your reflections with others brings growth in insight and depth of reflection. By all means, read the entire psalm thoughtfully sometime in the course of the week. Most of all, memorize. Remember, memory may someday be our only aid to prayer in times of difficulty or illness or distance from the normal routines of life.

So let's begin. Every one of us can be only as genuinely active as we are contemplative.

WEEK 27
DAY 1/*PSALM 18*

You, O God, are my lamp...
My God, who lightens my darkness.

Say the psalm verse over and over throughout the entire day until it becomes automatic, until it comes without effort, until you've memorized it.

DAY 2/*REFLECTION*.

Say the psalm verse to yourself thoughtfully several times. Now read the reflection and respond to it any way you can.

In some small mountain villages of Europe to this day, darkness is still a reality. But in most of Western society, it is difficult to realize what darkness really is or why the scriptures use it for a metaphor. We light our roads and our parking lots and our houses and our empty buildings 24 hours a day. Our big cities blaze throughout the night. But we have to know the meaning of darkness to understand the power of light.

Darkness is total blindness where certainty had been. Everyone will have an opportunity to experience darkness so they can come to know if Christ is their light. As long as confidence in God's will exists, we are in the light. As long as the things we think are light — education, money, friends, psychology, success — end with themselves, we are in darkness yet.

Question:

Name one darkness in your life that became light. How did that happen?

_____

_____

_____

DAY 3/*REFLECTION*. Read and respond.

A young rabbi said to the master, "You know when I study and when I join others in great feasts, I feel a great sense of light and life. But the minute it's over, it's all gone; everything dies in me."

The old rabbi replied: "It is just this feeling that happens when a person walks through the woods at night, when the breeze is cool and the scent in the air is delicious. If another joins the traveler with a lantern, they can walk safely and joyfully together. But if they come to a crossroads and the one with the lantern departs, then the first must grope her way alone unless she carries her light within her." *(Tales of the Hasidim)*

Question:

Do you travel by the light of another or do you carry a light within you? Or, do you do both? Explain. How can you keep the inner flame burning?

DAY 4/*PERSONAL REFLECTION.*

Now write your own insights or problems with this verse as diary or dialogue or testimony or debate. Write with feeling and with honesty.

You, O God, are my lamp...
  My God, who lightens my darkness.

DAY 5/*MEMORIZE.*

Write from memory the psalm verse you've been contemplating. (Remember the psalm number, too.)

_____
_____
_____
_____
_____

At this point in my life this psalm verse
_____
_____
_____
_____
_____
_____
_____
_____
_____
_____
_____
_____
_____
_____
_____

ACTION.
Find a dark spot. A totally dark spot. Stay there for awhile. Try to move around in it. Say the psalm verse over and over.

WEEK 28

DAY 1/*PSALM 77*

This is what causes my grief,
* That the way of the Most High has changed.*

Say the psalm verse over and over throughout the entire day until it becomes automatic, until it comes without effort, until you've memorized it.

DAY 2/*REFLECTION*

Say the psalm verse to yourself thoughtfully several times. Now read the reflection and respond to it any way you can.

This is a good psalm to say when we feel agitated. Like the psalmist, we don't want our plans changed either. The way things were, the way I say they should be, that's what we want. We get a plan — for work, for the day, for life — and we insist that that's the way things have to be. The truth is, though, that in most of the things of life, God has different designs for us. So, if we cling too fiercely to our limited vision, we break. On the other hand, if we meet God openheartedly, we find what the psalmist found: This is the God who works wonders.

Question:

Which of your plans are going awry? What wonder is coming out of it?

_____
_____
_____
_____
_____

DAY 3/*REFLECTION*. Read and respond.

A stream was working itself across the country, experiencing little difficulty. It ran around the rocks and through the mountains. Then it arrived at a desert. Just as it had crossed every other barrier, the stream tried to cross this one, but it found that as fast as it ran into the sand, its waters disappeared. After many attempts the stream became very discouraged. It appeared that there was no way it could continue the journey.

Then a voice came in the wind. "If you stay the way you are you cannot cross the sands, you cannot become more than a quagmire. To go further you will have to lose yourself."

"But if I lose myself," the stream cried, "I will never know what I'm supposed to be."

"Oh, on the contrary," said the voice. "If you lose yourself you will become more than you ever dreamed you could be."

So the stream surrendered to the drying sun. And the clouds into which it was formed were carried by the raging wind for many miles. Once it crossed the desert, the stream poured down from the skies, fresh and clean, and full of energy that comes from storms. (*adapted from the Sufi tales*)

Question:

This story (choose one): _____ makes me uneasy; _____ frightens me; _____ brings inner peace; _____ inspires me.

DAY 4/*PERSONAL REFLECTION.*

Now write your own insights or problems with this verse as diary or dialogue or testimony or debate. Write with feeling and with honesty.

This is what causes my grief,
   That the way of the Most High has changed.

DAY 5/*MEMORIZE*.

Write from memory the psalm verse you've been contemplating. (Remember the psalm number, too.)

_____
_____
_____
_____
_____

At this point in my life this psalm verse
_____
_____
_____
_____
_____
_____
_____
_____
_____
_____
_____
_____

ACTION.
Be part of life's wonders. Today give a small, but meaningful, present — some candy, a pack of gum, a plant, whatever — to someone who would never expect to get anything from you.

WEEK 29
DAY 1/*PSALM 49*

In their riches they lack wisdom;
  They take nothing with them when they die...

Say the psalm verse over and over throughout the entire day until it becomes automatic, until it comes without effort, until you've memorized it.

DAY 2/*REFLECTION*

Say the psalm verse to yourself thoughtfully several times. Now read the reflection and respond to it any way you can.

This psalm is a call to simplicity of life, and/but the important thing to realize is that the purpose of simplicity or poverty is not asceticism. The purpose of simplicity is contemplation: to remove the distractions that come from things for the pursuit and search for God.

But we rationalize. We struggle, too. We say since we have so little we have a right to a little better this, a little newer that, a few more of those. We hoard. We protect. We keep heaping things up that have no meaning.

Question:

Look around the room you're in or at the things you have with you. What is it that you feel you simply could not give away? Why?

_____
_____
_____
_____
_____

DAY 3/*REFLECTION*. Read and respond.

Ryokan, a Zen master, lived the simplest kind of life in a little hut at the foot of the mountain. One evening a thief visited the hut only to discover there was nothing to steal.

　Ryokan returned and caught him. "You may have come a long way to visit me," he told the prowler, "and you should not return empty-handed. Please take my clothes as a gift."

　The thief was bewildered. He took the clothes and slunk away.

　"Poor fellow," Ryokan mused. "I wish I could give him the beautiful moon."

Question:

List three adjectives that you would use to describe Ryokan. Explain your choices.

DAY 4/*PERSONAL REFLECTION.*

Now write your own insights or problems with this verse as diary or dialogue or testimony or debate. Write with feeling and with honesty.

In their riches they lack wisdom;
  They take nothing with them when they die...

DAY 5/*MEMORIZE.*

Write from memory the psalm verse you've been contemplating. (Remember the psalm number, too.)

_____
_____
_____
_____
_____

At this point in my life this psalm verse

_____
_____
_____
_____
_____
_____
_____
_____
_____
_____
_____
_____

ACTION.
Find a newspaper article or magazine piece, fiction or nonfiction, that gives an example of foolish accumulation or loss of perspective in life. Put it up someplace where you can see it for awhile.

WEEK 30

DAY 1/*PSALM 92*

It is good to give thanks to God.

Say the psalm verse over and over throughout the entire day until it becomes automatic, until it comes without effort, until you've memorized it.

DAY 2/*REFLECTION*

Say the psalm verse to yourself thoughtfully several times. Now read the reflection and respond to it any way you can.

Those who give thanks to God get a great deal more than they give.

The fact is that it is good psychologically to keep our thoughts light and full of praise because we feel the way we think. It is not true that we think the way we feel, so that if we control our negative thoughts we can control our negative feelings.

It's good spiritually, too, to give thanks to God because that is the beginning of contemplation. Even something as simple as being grateful for the wonders of natural things brings us to a sense of mindfulness that is of the essence of cosmic oneness.

Finally, it is good socially to have a spirit of thankfulness. It makes us a positive presence in a group. Only the negative want to be around the negative.

Today, stop and thank God, consciously, for the good things of the day.

Question:

List all the good things that happened to you today. Don't forget anything, e.g., a glass of cold water, etc.

_____

_____

_____

DAY 3/*REFLECTION*. Read and respond.

According to medieval legend, God once sent two messengers to earth on a special mission, giving each a basket. One angel was assigned to gather all the prayers of petition and the second angel all the prayers of thanksgiving.

The first seraph returned shortly with a basket overflowing with requests. "God's people have remembered well the Bible's counsel, 'Ask and you shall receive,'" reported the angel. The other angel, however, was gone a very long time and when she finally arrived back in heaven, her basket was nearly empty. "I had great difficulty finding Christians who express prayers of thanksgiving," said the spirit sadly.

Question:

Try to recall your personal prayer during the past week. Is this story true in your life? How do you pray most often — from a posture of petition or a posture of thanksgiving?

DAY 4/*PERSONAL REFLECTION.*

Now write your own insights or problems with this verse as diary or dialogue or testimony or debate. Write with feeling and with honesty.

It is good to give thanks to God.

DAY 5/*MEMORIZE.*

Write from memory the psalm verse you've been contemplating. (Remember the psalm number, too.)

_____
_____
_____
_____
_____

At this point in my life this psalm verse

_____
_____
_____
_____
_____
_____
_____
_____
_____
_____
_____
_____
_____

ACTION.

With your eyes closed, open up your photograph album to three different photos. What person are you thankful for in each of the pictures? Send at least one of them a greeting card.

WEEK 31

DAY 1/PSALM 46

Be still and know that I am God.

Say the psalm verse over and over throughout the entire day until it becomes automatic, until it comes without effort, until you've memorized it.

DAY 2/REFLECTION

Say the psalm verse to yourself thoughtfully several times. Now read the reflection and respond to it any way you can.

T he condition that the psalm puts on the experience is stillness. We need to experiment with the meaning of that. We have to learn to pause, to simply be still. It's an antidote to letting business become all of life. It's a way to live the active life contemplatively by listening, by simply stopping everything for 60 seconds a day, by quieting ourselves so that we bring gentleness and quiet into a loud and distracted world, by acknowledging interiorly, consciously, often, that God is God in the face of the fact that most of the time we really think *we* are.

Question:

Write down what you hear around you right now. Then close your eyes and listen. What did you hear this time? Was it different from other occasions? Why?

_____
_____
_____
_____
_____
_____
_____

DAY 3/*REFLECTION*. Read and respond.

Here in the palm of my hand is a hazelnut,
a small thing, round like a ball.
It is all that is made; it is made by Love
See in this little thing three truths:
God made it, God loves it, God keeps it.
In these truths stay and grow.

You will have pain and affliction,
trouble and strain and doubt.
But you shall not be overcome and all shall be well.
Yes, all shall be well,
and all will be well,
and thou shalt see thyself
that all manner of thing
shall be well.
(extract from "A Julian of Norwich Dialogue" — *A Light in the Darkness*)

Question:

Can you say of yourself what Julian said of the hazelnut: God made it, God loves it, God keeps it.

_____
_____
_____
_____
_____
_____
_____
_____
_____
_____

DAY 4/PERSONAL REFLECTION.

Now write your own insights or problems with this verse as diary or dialogue or testimony or debate. Write with feeling and with honesty.

Be still and know that I am God.

DAY 5/*MEMORIZE*.

Write from memory the psalm verse you've been contemplating. (Remember the psalm number, too.)

_____
_____
_____
_____
_____

At this point in my life this psalm verse

_____
_____
_____
_____
_____
_____
_____
_____
_____
_____
_____
_____
_____
_____

ACTION.
Don't turn on the radio, the TV, the record player or the clock radio for one night.

WEEK 32
DAY 1/*PSALM 19*

Day after day takes up the story;
  night after night makes known the
message.

Say the psalm verse over and over throughout the entire day until it becomes automatic, until it comes without effort, until you've memorized it.

DAY 2/*REFLECTION.*

Say the psalm verse to yourself thoughtfully several times. Now read the reflection and respond to it any way you can.

O ur part in creation, as a truly priestly people, is simply this: to be the living proof that Jesus is and saves and cares through us. But to do that well, it must be done with a real sense of purpose. Once I'm not in a thing for myself alone, my decisions and attitudes and positions will change.

That takes courage. Others may often call us foolish for our efforts.

That takes trust and a sense of risk. To be a sign that Jesus is and saves and cares for us all will cost.

But that is our real call. There is no other.

Question:

What one thing have you done for someone who is not an American and does not live in this country?

_____
_____
_____
_____
_____

DAY 3/*REFLECTION*. Read and respond.

If you are neutral in situations of injustice, you have chosen the side of the oppressor. If an elephant has his foot on the tail of a mouse and you say that you are neutral, the mouse will not appreciate your neutrality. (Bishop Desmond Tutu)

Question:

Name three situations of injustice in today's world. Are you helping the "elephant" or the "mouse"?

DAY 4/*PERSONAL REFLECTION.*

Now write your own insights or problems with this verse as diary or dialogue or testimony or debate. Write with feeling and with honesty.

Day after day takes up the story; night after night makes known the message.

DAY 5/*MEMORIZE*.

Write from memory the psalm verse you've been contemplating. (Remember the psalm number, too.)

_____
_____
_____
_____

At this point in my life this psalm verse

_____
_____
_____
_____
_____
_____
_____
_____
_____
_____
_____
_____
_____

ACTION.
Go out of your way to make friends with someone who has only recently arrived in this country or write a letter to someone in Russia saying that you do not want our countries to be enemies.

WEEK 33

DAY 1/*PSALM 36*

*In you is the source of life
and in your light we see light.*

Say the psalm verse over and over throughout the entire day until it becomes automatic, until it comes without effort, until you've memorized it.

DAY 2/*REFLECTION*.

Say the psalm verse to yourself thoughtfully several times. Now read the reflection and respond to it any way you can.

T his is a good verse to remember when we feel our energy flagging. Or we begin to think that we can't do one more thing. Or we're sure we simply cannot do what is expected of us now. All of those moments in life are opportunities to realize that energy comes from right-mindedness and is sapped by anxiety and compulsion and drivenness. If we can live trusting the will of God for us in the present moment, we will have all the energy we need. Why? Because doing the will of God is the source of life for us. Why? Because it is the light of what is important in God's sight that brings light to our own confusion and choices and conflicts.

Question:

What things am I emphasizing in my life right now? Are they the right things or the wrong things? Are they bringing life and light? If not, why not?

_____

_____

_____

DAY 3/*REFLECTION*. Read and respond.

A monk was once asked, "What do you do there in the monastery?" He replied: "We fall and get up, fall and get up, fall and get up again."

Question:

Does this story encourage or discourage you? Explain.

DAY 4/*PERSONAL REFLECTION.*

Now write your own insights or problems with this verse as diary or dialogue or testimony or debate. Write with feeling and with honesty.

*In you is the source of life
and in your light we see light.*

DAY 5/*MEMORIZE.*

Write from memory the psalm verse you've been contemplating. (Remember the psalm number, too.)

_____
_____
_____
_____
_____
_____

At this point in my life this psalm verse

_____
_____
_____
_____
_____
_____
_____
_____
_____
_____
_____
_____
_____
_____
_____

ACTION.
Select any picture in any magazine. How is it like or unlike your life? Is that good or bad and why?

WEEK 34

DAY 1/*PSALM 59*

O my strength, it is you to whom I turn.
For you, O God, are my stronghold.

Say the psalm verse over and over throughout the entire day until it becomes automatic, until it comes without effort, until you've memorized it.

DAY 2/*REFLECTION*.

Say the psalm verse to yourself thoughtfully several times. Now read the reflection and respond to it any way you can.

This is a psalm about spiritual maturity. It confronts us with a serious question. When hard things happen, to what do I turn? To people to change them for me? To things to distract myself? To petty satisfactions to make me feel better? To complaining and whining and manipulative behavior to make others do what I want them to do? There's no spiritual maturity in that. Spiritual maturity depends on staying intent on the real purpose and meaning of life.

Spiritual immaturity is to look as if God matters, but to care only for myself. Spiritual immaturity is to say that others matter but to design my world around myself. Spiritual immaturity is to go through the motions of prayer but to be so far from the things of the spirit that I don't even know how far away I am. Spiritual immaturity is to play at being spiritual but to avoid as far as possible what it takes to be simple, to be loving, to be present to God and so to those who need me.

Spiritual maturity keeps things in perspective and turns always to God. I have to trust others and trust God. Then God can work in my life; then I can allow change to change me.

Question:

What am I resisting in life right now? Why?

DAY 3/REFLECTION. Read and respond.

A seeker went to visit the Sage hoping for enlightenment. The Sage invited the seeker into her cell and offered her a drink. "Yes," a drink would be fine," said the seeker.

The Sage poured until the seeker's glass was full and then kept pouring. The seeker watched until she could take it no longer. "It is overfull," the seeker said, "no more will go in."

"Like the glass," the Sage said, "you are full of your own truths, ideas and opinions. You cannot be enlightened until you first empty your glass."

Question:

Imagine emptying a glass filled with your ideas, opinions and truths. What would pour out?

DAY 4/PERSONAL REFLECTION.

Now write your own insights or problems with this verse as diary or dialogue or testimony or debate. Write with feeling and with honesty.

O my strength, it is you to whom I turn.
For you, O God, are my stronghold.

DAY 5/*MEMORIZE.*

Write from memory the psalm verse you've been contemplating. (Remember the psalm number, too.)

_____
_____
_____
_____
_____

At this point in my life this psalm verse

_____
_____
_____
_____
_____
_____
_____
_____
_____
_____
_____
_____
_____
_____

ACTION.
Make a visit to a church or chapel or simply get down on your knees at home. Pray for the strength to accept the will of God for you in whatever difficulty is facing you right now.

WEEK 35
DAY 1/*PSALM 63*

Your love is better than life. . . .
*   My soul is filled as with a banquet;*
My life is full of joy.

Say the psalm verse over and over throughout the entire day until it becomes automatic, until it comes without effort, until you've memorized it.

DAY 2/*REFLECTION*.

Say the psalm verse to yourself thoughtfully several times. Now read the reflection and respond to it any way you can.

We spend so much time wanting things to be better that we fail to see our real gifts. We don't enjoy the banquets in our life because we are always grasping for something more: the perfect schedule, the perfect work, the perfect friend, the perfect community. We have to realize that God's gifts are all around us, that joy is an attitude of mind, an awareness that my life is basically good. Dissatisfaction is often a sign of something wrong in me.

Question:

Name three things that are bad in your life right now. Name six things that are good.

_____
_____
_____
_____
_____
_____

DAY 3/*REFLECTION*. Read and respond.

A rabbi in a dream found himself in heaven. "Where is paradise?," he asked. So they showed him a room where many spiritual leaders were sitting around a table absorbed in the scriptures. "Is this, then, all there is to paradise?," he queried in disappointment. "You do not understand," they said to him. "The sages are not in paradise. Paradise is in the sages." *(Tales of the Hasidim)*

Question:

With this psalm journal you have been spending time with the scriptures. Has there been "any taste of paradise"? Explain.

DAY 4/*PERSONAL REFLECTION.*

Now write your own insights or problems with this verse as diary or dialogue or testimony or debate. Write with feeling and with honesty.

Your love is better than life...
  My soul is filled as with a banquet;
My life is full of joy.

DAY 5/*MEMORIZE.*

Write from memory the psalm verse you've been contemplating. (Remember the psalm number, too.)

_____
_____
_____
_____
_____

At this point in my life this psalm verse

_____
_____
_____
_____
_____
_____
_____
_____
_____
_____
_____
_____
_____
_____
_____

ACTION.
Take a picture of something that was difficult for you to deal with in life but which you came to value. Carry it in your wallet.

WEEK 36

DAY 1/*PSALM 38*

My God, do not stay far off.

Say the psalm verse over and over throughout the entire day until it becomes automatic, until it comes without effort, until you've memorized it.

DAY 2/*REFLECTION.*

Say the psalm verse to yourself thoughtfully several times. Now read the reflection and respond to it any way you can.

The beautiful thing about prayer is that, in the instant that we begin to pray, God is no longer distant. We say the spiritual life seems barren when what we mean is that we have gone through the motions of the spiritual life but not into it. We know about ritual but not about response. We say, "I tried to pray but nothing happened and so I quit." And that's exactly why nothing happens.

The oldest truth of the spiritual life is that I have to put myself in the presence of God. Put yourself. Think. Answer.

Question:

Is God close to you or far away? What stops you from putting yourself in the presence of God?

DAY 3/*REFLECTION*. Read and respond.

God decided to reveal himself to a king and a peasant. He sent an angel to inform them of the blessed news.

"Oh king," the angel announced, "God has deigned to reveal himself to you in whatever manner you wish. In what form do you want him to appear?"

Seated on his throne and surrounded by awestruck subjects, the king proclaimed, "How else would I wish to see God, save in his majesty and power? Show him to us in the full glory of his kingship!"

God granted this wish and appeared as a bolt of lightning that instantly pulverized the king and his court. Nothing, not even a cinder, remained.

The angel then manifested himself to a peasant, saying: "God deigns to reveal himself to you in whatever manner you desire. How do you wish to see God?"

Scratching his head and puzzling a long while, the peasant finally said, "I am a poor man and not worthy to see God face to face. But if it is his will to show himself to me, let it be in those things with which I am familiar. Let me see God in the earth I plow, the water I drink, the food I eat. Let me see God in the faces of my family and neighbors."

God granted the peasant his wish, and he lived a long and happy life. May God grant you the same!

Question:

Name three circumstances, places, persons in which you have difficulty seeing the face of God. Spend some time with your reflection.

_____
_____
_____
_____

DAY 4/*PERSONAL REFLECTION*.

Now write your own insights or problems with this verse as diary or dialogue or testimony or debate. Write with feeling and with honesty.

My God, do not stay far off.

DAY 5/*MEMORIZE.*

Write from memory the psalm verse you've been contemplating. (Remember the psalm number, too.)

_____
_____
_____
_____
_____
_____

At this point in my life this psalm verse

_____
_____
_____
_____
_____
_____
_____
_____
_____
_____
_____
_____
_____
_____

ACTION.

Find a picture of someone who was difficult for you to come to know but whom you came to value. Carry it in your wallet with this psalm verse written on the back to remind you that God is waiting to get to know you, too.

WEEK 37
DAY 1/PSALM 122

For love of my family and friends I say: "Peace upon you..."

Say the psalm verse over and over throughout the entire day until it becomes automatic, until it comes without effort, until you've memorized it.

DAY 2/REFLECTION.

Say the psalm verse to yourself thoughtfully several times. Now read the reflection and respond to it any way you can.

This psalm puts on us the burden, the gift of wishing everyone well, of wanting everyone to prosper, to succeed, to be happy. Why? Because the happiness of others in our community is key to our own happiness: It's good for the environment. This psalm teaches us what it is to call a blessing down on others. In doing so, we show we are willing to see that others are blessed. It also helps us to realize that every blessing given to another is in some way a blessing on us, too.

Question:

Is there anyone you know for whom you do not sincerely want peace? Is there anyone you know that you would deliberately ignore or aggravate? Is there anyone you know that you would not exert yourself to help? What has been the effect of that?

DAY 3/*REFLECTION*. Read and respond.

Let peacemakers remember, let them above all remember that it is no manner of good preaching peace unless we preach the things that make for peace. (Eric Gill)

Question:
What things make for peace? List five.

DAY 4/*PERSONAL REFLECTION.*

Now write your own insights or problems with this verse as diary or dialogue or testimony or debate. Write with feeling and with honesty.

For love of my family and friends I say: "Peace upon you..."

DAY 5/*MEMORIZE*.

Write from memory the psalm verse you've been contemplating. (Remember the psalm number, too.)

_____
_____
_____
_____
_____

At this point in my life this psalm verse

_____
_____
_____
_____
_____
_____
_____
_____
_____
_____
_____
_____
_____
_____
_____

ACTION.
Tonight call someone who is facing a challenge of some kind. Call down a blessing upon them, i.e., wish them well and offer to do something specific to help them.

WEEK 38

DAY 1/*PSALM 21*

In you our ancestors put their trust;
They trusted and you set them free...

Say the psalm verse over and over throughout the entire day until it becomes automatic, until it comes without effort, until you've memorized it.

DAY 2/*REFLECTION.*

Say the psalm verse to yourself thoughtfully several times. Now read the reflection and respond to it any way you can.

This psalm remembers good times in bad times. It talks about being saved — from dogs and lions and oxen, from irrational, unreasonable obstacles. In other words, it reminds us that we can't talk our way out of some things, such as poor health or error or human fault. In all these things, the psalmist says, it is trust, not necessarily a change of circumstances, that sets us free. But we so often resist, despite the fact that the past has always worked to our good. Everyone has something in life to face, to work through in order to be free, to be authentic. The answer is to trust. Simple?

Question:

What is happening in my life now that requires a great deal of trust?

_____
_____
_____
_____
_____
_____

DAY 3/*REFLECTION*. Read and respond.

I don't know who — or what — put the question. I don't know when it was put. I don't even remember answering. But at some moment I did answer *yes* to Someone — or Something — and from that hour I was certain that existence is meaningful and that, therefore, my life, in self-surrender, has a goal.

From that moment I have known what it means, "not to look back," and "to take no thought for the morrow." (Dag Hammarskjold)

Question:

Have you said *yes* to Someone or Something? How do you know?

_____
_____
_____
_____
_____
_____
_____
_____
_____
_____
_____
_____
_____
_____
_____
_____
_____
_____

DAY 4/*PERSONAL REFLECTION.*

Now write your own insights or problems with this verse as diary or dialogue or testimony or debate. Write with feeling and with honesty.

In you our ancestors put their trust;
  They trusted and you set them free...

DAY 5/*MEMORIZE*.

Write from memory the psalm verse you've been contemplating. (Remember the psalm number, too.)

_____
_____
_____
_____
_____

At this point in my life this psalm verse

_____
_____
_____
_____
_____
_____
_____
_____
_____
_____
_____
_____
_____
_____
_____

ACTION.
Write about some circumstance in the history of an older person in your family. Did your ancestors put their trust in God?

WEEK 39

DAY 1/*PSALM 26*

*Examine me, O God, and try me;
O test my heart and my mind...*

Say the psalm verse over and over throughout the entire day until it becomes automatic, until it comes without effort, until you've memorized it.

DAY 2/*REFLECTION*

Say the psalm verse to yourself thoughtfully several times. Now read the reflection and respond to it any way you can.

The psalm is very clear about the spiritual life: It is definitely not lived by those who say "Lord, Lord..." or those who only multiply prayers or rituals. Those who know that their love of God will be tried and who are open to that become spiritual giants. They know that commitment to the spiritual life costs. They who know that spirituality is a choice, not simply emotional comfort, will go down into the mind of God.

Question:

Are your mind and heart in tension right now? Do you know one thing but feel another? What is being tested in you?

DAY 3/*REFLECTION*. Read and respond.

The Peace Corps left today and my heart sank low. The danger is extreme and they were right to leave. . . . Now I must assess my own position, because I am not up for suicide. Several times I have decided to leave. I almost could except for the children, the poor bruised victims of adult lunacy. Who would care for them? Whose heart would be so staunch as to favor the reasonable thing in a sea of tears and helplessness? Not mine, dear friend, not mine. (From a letter of Jean Donovan, lay missioner murdered in El Salvador, 1980)

Question:

Do you care for the "children of the world"? Those hungry in Ethiopia? Those terrified in El Salvador? Those threatened with nuclear annihilation? Those yet unborn? How do you show your care?

DAY 4/*PERSONAL REFLECTION.*

Now write your own insights or problems with this verse as diary or dialogue or testimony or debate. Write with feeling and with honesty.

Examine me, O God, and try me;
 O test my heart and my mind...

DAY 5/*MEMORIZE*.

Write from memory the psalm verse you've been contemplating. (Remember the psalm number, too.)

_____
_____
_____
_____
_____
_____

At this point in my life this psalm verse

_____
_____
_____
_____
_____
_____
_____
_____
_____
_____
_____
_____
_____
_____
_____
_____

ACTION.
Name a spiritual giant in your life. Draw a picture or a symbol of what this person taught you about being open to God.

WEEK 40

DAY 1/PSALM 30

O Lord, you have raised my soul from the dead and restored me to life.

Say the psalm verse over and over throughout the entire day until it becomes automatic, until it comes without effort, until you've memorized it.

DAY 2/REFLECTION

Say the psalm verse to yourself thoughtfully several times. Now read the reflection and respond to it any way you can.

Souls often die before bodies do. We think we're not worth much because of what we do, or how old we are, or what we wear, or what our bodies are like. Sexism, racism, being "macho" oil the consumer society. We buy to look better, tougher, richer, or because we get constant messages of our inferiority and nothingness. When we combat the power of these things over us, our souls rise from the dead. We get life. We become persons. We become free. We set our minds and hearts on higher things. We become more than beings trapped by social norms. We become more than Xerox copies of a stereotype that looks and thinks and does what trend-setters say we must be. We must be centered people who are satisfied with ourselves and who want to become what God wants us to be.

Question:

What did I think about most yesterday? Is it life-giving or is it smothering the soul?

_____
_____
_____
_____

DAY 3/*REFLECTION*. Read and respond.

Someone was drawing water and my teacher placed my hand under the spout. As the cool stream gushed over one hand she spelled into the other the word water, first slowly, then rapidly. I stood still, my whole attention fixed upon the motion of her fingers. Suddenly I felt a misty consciousness as of something forgotten — a thrill of returning thought; and somehow the mystery of language was revealed to me. I knew that "w-a-t-e-r" meant the wonderful cool something that was flowing over my hand. The living word awakened my soul; gave it light, hope, joy, set it free. (Helen Keller, *The Story of My Life*)

Question:

Name one resurrection moment in your life — a time when you came to new awareness.

DAY 4/PERSONAL REFLECTION.

Now write your own insights or problems with this verse as diary or dialogue or testimony or debate. Write with feeling and with honesty.

O Lord, you have raised my soul from the dead and restored me to life.

DAY 5/*MEMORIZE*.

Write from memory the psalm verse you've been contemplating. (Remember the psalm number, too.)

_____
_____
_____
_____
_____

At this point in my life this psalm verse

_____
_____
_____
_____
_____
_____
_____
_____
_____
_____
_____
_____
_____

ACTION.
Find a good poem; memorize it. Learn to hum a classical piece. Do something that stretches your soul beyond dailiness.

WEEK 41

DAY 1 / PSALM 32

I kept my sin secret and my frame was wasted.
Day and night your hand was heavy upon me.

Say the psalm verse over and over throughout the entire day until it becomes automatic, until it comes without effort, until you've memorized it.

DAY 2 / REFLECTION.

Say the psalm verse to yourself thoughtfully several times. Now read the reflection and respond to it any way you can.

This psalm is a piece of very good psychology about the burdens we carry within us, our unforgiven sins.

We refuse to accept ourselves when we don't face our faults, our problems, our weaknesses, our angers, our sense of inadequacy. Even worse is blaming our problems on others, denying we have any, or insisting that we need to be perfect. Every doctor and psychologist in the country sees the effect of that in their offices every day.

We all have things we need to forgive in ourselves or face in ourselves. We have things we know we ought to ask forgiveness for from someone else but pride and stubbornness hold us back.

These things become a barrier between us and the community, a hot stone in the pit of the stomach, a block to real happiness. And nothing is going to get better until we face them.

Question:

What would you like to accept in yourself? What particular situation should you be asking forgiveness for from someone else?

DAY 3/*REFLECTION*. Read and respond.

I have always overshadowed Jonas with My mercy... Have you had sight of Me, Jonas My child? Mercy within mercy within mercy." (Thomas Merton, *The Sign of Jonas*)

Question:

Substitute your name for "Jonas." Now repeat the quote. Do you experience God as "mercy within mercy within mercy"?

DAY 4/*PERSONAL REFLECTION*.

Now write your own insights or problems with this verse as diary or dialogue or testimony or debate. Write with feeling and with honesty.

I kept my sin secret and my frame was wasted.
Day and night your hand was heavy upon me.

DAY 5/*MEMORIZE.*

Write from memory the psalm verse you've been contemplating. (Remember the psalm number, too.)

At this point in my life this psalm verse

ACTION.
When someone apologizes to you, say, "Thanks so much for being concerned. Don't give it another thought." (Feels good, doesn't it? That's what God is like.)

WEEK 42

DAY 1/*PSALM 35*

O God, say to my soul,
  I am your salvation...

Say the psalm verse over and over throughout the entire day until it becomes automatic, until it comes without effort, until you've memorized it.

DAY 2/*REFLECTION*.

Say the psalm verse to yourself thoughtfully several times. Now read the reflection and respond to it any way you can.

This is a moody psalm about the ups and down of life:

Some days we are sure of our blessings; other days we are full of depression;

Some days we're certain we're loved; other days we feel distant from everyone;

Some days everything goes my way; other days nothing I do turns out right;

Some days my faith is strong; other days I wallow in despair.

In those times, I need to remember Psalm 35 and pray for a consciousness of the presence of God. When I am thinking most about myself, when self has become the only filter through which I see the world, I need to stretch my vision.

Question:

What is capturing all my attention today? Write about it and then end your paragraph with the psalm verse as an exercise in perspective.

DAY 3/*REFLECTION*. Read and respond.

The day of my spiritual awakening was the day I saw all things in God and God in all things. (Mechtild of Magdenburg)

Question:
Have you had a day of spiritual awakening? Can you share it?

DAY 4/*PERSONAL REFLECTION.*

Now write your own insights or problems with this verse as diary or dialogue or testimony or debate. Write with feeling and with honesty.

O God, say to my soul,
  I am your salvation...

DAY 5/*MEMORIZE.*

Write from memory the psalm verse you've been contemplating. (Remember the psalm number, too.)

_____
_____
_____
_____
_____

At this point in my life this psalm verse

_____
_____
_____
_____
_____
_____
_____
_____
_____
_____
_____
_____
_____
_____

ACTION.

Draw a graph of your life in the last month or year. Mark the ups and downs. What were they? Why were they?

WEEK 43
DAY 1/*PSALM 51*

Purify me, then I shall be clean...
Put a steadfast spirit within me.

Say the psalm verse over and over throughout the entire day until it becomes automatic, until it comes without effort, until you've memorized it.

DAY 2/*REFLECTION*

Say the psalm verse to yourself thoughtfully several times. Now read the reflection and respond to it any way you can.

We all want to do the discipline we want to do. We choose our penances. The ultimate penance, however, may be simply to learn from life and not to run away from its message for me. Prayer is the struggle to know the will of God in life, to realize that both the journey and the kingdom are right here. The challenges we face in life right now are what will purify us of our selfishness and our self-centeredness. God knows what each of us needs to do to be spiritually whole: to reconcile, perhaps; to pray in a way that leads to action and to act out of a sense of prayer; to give our natural gifts for the sake of others; to learn from one another; to live for something larger than ourselves — recklessly, totally and without counting time or comparing effort.

What we have to do, in other words, is to accept life as it is — as the raw material of our growth, development and commitment. Nothing is ever wasted. Out of every experience comes a new kind of synergy. Be patient, pilgrim.

Question:

What is purifying you right now? Is your spirit steadfast enough to weather it well? Why or why not?

DAY 3/*REFLECTION*. Read and respond.

During World War II, a German widow hid Jewish refugees in her own home. As her friends discovered the situation, they became extremely alarmed.

"You are risking your own well-being," they told her.

"I know that," she said.

"Then why," they demanded, "do you persist in this foolishness?"

Her answer was stark and to the point. "I am doing it," she said, "because the time is now and I am here."

Question:

Each of us also stands in a time and place. Where is life being threatened today? How are you responding? Like the widow? Like her friends?

DAY 4/*PERSONAL REFLECTION*.

Now write your own insights or problems with this verse as diary or dialogue or testimony or debate. Write with feeling and with honesty.

Purify me, then I shall be clean...
 Put a steadfast spirit within me.

DAY 5/*MEMORIZE.*

Write from memory the psalm verse you've been contemplating. (Remember the psalm number, too.)

At this point in my life this psalm verse

ACTION.
Whatever the weather is — hot, rainy, cold, windy — go out and stand in it for 10 minutes. Let it affect you. What good came from the experience?

WEEK 44
DAY 1/*PSALM 61*

On the rock too high for me to reach, set me on high.

Say the psalm verse over and over throughout the entire day until it becomes automatic, until it comes without effort, until you've memorized it.

DAY 2/*REFLECTION*

Say the psalm verse to yourself thoughtfully several times. Now read the reflection and respond to it any way you can.

The simplicity of the statement is its power. The psalmist prays for us: "Give me what I need — even when I don't know what to ask for and couldn't do it for myself, even if I knew." But the action of God is not always spectacular. It is, in fact, usually in the ordinary events of life, even in scripture. Nor is it true that God always and only acts through good things.

So, it is good to wonder what "rock too high for me" God is trying to set me on now. Spiritual growth implies that I ask: Am I resisting? Am I scattered and unaware? What is the word of God for me in my present difficulties or struggles? Then I have to allow God to work in my life.

Question:

What "rock too high for you" have you already been set on in life? What has happened to you that you couldn't have possibly done for yourself?

DAY 3/*REFLECTION*. Read and respond.

A seeker searched for years to know the secret of achievement and success in human life. One night in a dream a sage appeared bearing the answer to the secret.

The sage said simply, "Stretch out your hand and reach what you can."

"No, it can't be that," said the seeker. "It must be something harder, something more satisfying to the human spirit."

The sage replied softly, "You are right, it is something harder. It is this: Stretch out your hand and reach what you cannot."

Question:

Think back on your life. List all the things that at one time you thought were impossible to reach and are now within easy grasp, e.g., a new skill, a better diet, a virtue. Are you reaching for anything now? What?

DAY 4/*PERSONAL REFLECTION.*

Now write your own insights or problems with this verse as diary or dialogue or testimony or debate. Write with feeling and with honesty.

On the rock too high for me to reach, set me on high.

DAY 5/*MEMORIZE*.

Write from memory the psalm verse you've been contemplating. (Remember the psalm number, too.)

_____
_____
_____
_____
_____

At this point in my life this psalm verse

_____
_____
_____
_____
_____
_____
_____
_____
_____
_____
_____
_____
_____
_____
_____

ACTION.
What are you committed to that does not seem to be working? Go back and try it one more time.

WEEK 45
DAY 1/PSALM 71

I will always hope and praise you more and more.

Say the psalm verse over and over throughout the entire day until it becomes automatic, until it comes without effort, until you've memorized it.

DAY 2/REFLECTION.

Say the psalm verse to yourself thoughtfully several times. Now read the reflection and respond to it any way you can.

Hope is not the expectation of life without struggle. Hope is the certainty that even in struggle God is there.

Question:

What was the greatest experience of hope in your life?

DAY 3/*REFLECTION*. Read and respond.

Saint Augustine says that of the three theological virtues, hope is the greatest. Faith only tells us that God is and love tells us that God is good, but hope tells us that God will work God's will. Augustine continues: "Hope has two lovely daughters: anger and courage. Anger so that what must not be may not be; courage so that what should be can be."

Question:

Name the most hopeful person you know. What do you think sustains that person's hope?

DAY 4/*PERSONAL REFLECTION*.

Now write your own insights or problems with this verse as diary or dialogue or testimony or debate. Write with feeling and with honesty.

I will always hope and praise you more and more.

DAY 5/*MEMORIZE*.

Write from memory the psalm verse you've been contemplating. (Remember the psalm number, too.)

At this point in my life this psalm verse

ACTION.
Talk to the most hopeful person you know. Ask them what sustains their hope.

WEEK 46

DAY 1/*PSALM 94*

*O Lord, avenging God,
   Avenging God, appear.*

Say the psalm verse over and over throughout the entire day until it becomes automatic, until it comes without effort, until you've memorized it.

DAY 2/*REFLECTION*.

Say the psalm verse to yourself thoughtfully several times. Now read the reflection and respond to it any way you can.

This is a psalm to remember in the midst of difficult situations. It sounds harsh but it is really a lesson in reliance on God rather than a commitment to personal revenge. The psalmist says that God, not I, must repay any ill will done to me.

Consequently, I don't have to wear myself out on malice or plotting or pouting or secret grudges over things that seem to have no resolution.

The lesson is that it's better to trust our hurts to God than to carry in our hearts the acid that will eventually destroy only ourselves.

Question:

Have you ever harbored deep resentfulness against anyone? What stopped you from putting it down?

_____
_____
_____
_____

DAY 3/*REFLECTION*. Read and respond.

Once there was a very old man who used to meditate early every morning under a large tree on the bank of the Ganges river in India. One morning, having finished his meditation, the old man opened his eyes and saw a scorpion floating helplessly in the strong current of the river. As the scorpion was pulled closer to the tree, it got caught in the long tree roots that branched out far into the river. The scorpion struggled frantically to free itself but got more and more entangled in the complex network of the tree roots.

When the old man saw this, he immediately stretched himself onto the extended roots and reached out to rescue the drowning scorpion. But as soon as he touched it, the animal jerked and stung him wildly. Instinctively, the man withdrew his hand, but then, having regained his balance, he once again stretched himself out along the roots to save the agonized scorpion. But every time the old man came within reach, the scorpion stung him so badly with its poisonous tail that his hands became bloody and his face distorted by pain.

At that moment, a passerby saw the old man stretched out on the roots struggling with the scorpion and shouted, "Hey, stupid old man. What's wrong with you? Only a fool risks his life for the sake of an ugly, useless creature. Don't you know that you may kill yourself to save that ungrateful animal?"

Slowly the old man turned his head and looking calmly in the stranger's eyes, he said, "Friend, because it is the nature of the scorpion to sting, why should I give up my own nature to save?"

Question:

Have you ever been "stung" by something you tried to help? What was your reaction?

_____
_____
_____
_____
_____
_____

DAY 4/*PERSONAL REFLECTION.*

Now write your own insights or problems with this verse as diary or dialogue or testimony or debate. Write with feeling and with honesty.

O Lord, avenging God,
 Avenging God, appear.

DAY 5/*MEMORIZE*.

Write from memory the psalm verse you've been contemplating. (Remember the psalm number, too.)

_____
_____
_____
_____
_____
_____

At this point in my life this psalm verse

_____
_____
_____
_____
_____
_____
_____
_____
_____
_____
_____
_____
_____
_____
_____
_____
_____
_____

ACTION.
Send a card to someone who would have been your enemy if you had not reached out to that person.

WEEK 47

DAY 1/PSALM 144

*God is my rock, my refuge and my fortress;
my stronghold, my deliverer,
my shield in whom I trust.*

Say the psalm verse over and over throughout the entire day until it becomes automatic, until it comes without effort, until you've memorized it.

DAY 2/REFLECTION

Say the psalm verse to yourself thoughtfully several times. Now read the reflection and respond to it any way you can.

The psalms are songs for the whole people. Many of them are patriotic songs of the community, not just the experience of a single person. In these songs, God's will was always above national interests even when that *will* was that the nation was punished. The psalms always acknowledged national sin.

The Christian nation — this nation that calls itself Christian — has a lot to learn from the psalms about national morality and national values. Is God really above national culture in our lives? If so, we should be devoted to world development, not "Americanism."

Question:

Name a national policy you believe may be destructive of another nation or people that you have not remarked about to anyone. Why not?

_____

_____

_____

DAY 3/*REFLECTION*. Read and respond.

One day a young fugitive, trying to hide himself from the enemy, entered a small village. The people were kind to him and offered him a place to stay. But when the soldiers who sought the fugitive asked where he was hiding, everyone became very fearful. The soldiers threatened to burn the village and kill every person in it unless the young man was handed over to them before dawn. The people went to the minister and asked him what to do. The minister, torn between handing over the boy to the enemy or having his people killed, withdrew to his room and read his Bible, hoping to find an answer before dawn. After many hours, in the early morning his eyes fell on these words: "It is better that one man dies than that the whole people be lost."

Then the minister closed the Bible, called the soldiers and told them where the boy was hidden. And after the soldiers led the fugitive away to be killed, there was a feast in the village because the minister had saved the lives of the people. But the minister did not celebrate. Overcome with a deep sadness, he remained in his room. That night an angel came to him and asked, "What have you done?" He said, "I handed over the fugitive to the enemy." Then the angel said: "But don't you know that you have handed over the messiah?" "How could I know?," the minister replied anxiously. Then the angel said, "If, instead of reading your Bible, you had visited this young man just once and looked into his eyes, you would have known."

Question:

Where does your sympathy lie? With the fugitive? With the minister? With the people? Who or what are you prepared to sacrifice in order to save the nation? Have you ever had an "enemy" that became a friend when you looked into his or her eyes or called them by name? Have you ever looked, really looked, into the faces of those the government has labeled "enemy"?

_____

_____

_____

DAY 4/*PERSONAL REFLECTION*.

Now write your own insights or problems with this verse as diary or dialogue or testimony or debate. Write with feeling and with honesty.

God is my rock, my refuge and my fortress; my stronghold, my deliverer, my shield in whom I trust.

DAY 5/*MEMORIZE*.

Write from memory the psalm verse you've been contemplating. (Remember the psalm number, too.)

At this point in my life this psalm verse

ACTION.
Send a postcard to the president asking him to increase American efforts to curb world hunger.

WEEK 48

DAY 1 / PSALM 90

*Give us joy to balance our affliction,
for the years when we knew misfortune.*

Say the psalm verse over and over throughout the entire day until it becomes automatic, until it comes without effort, until you've memorized it.

DAY 2 / REFLECTION.

Say the psalm verse to yourself thoughtfully several times. Now read the reflection and respond to it any way you can.

This psalm seems fair enough. All we want is for good times and bad times to at least come out even. We're not asking for easy street. It does expose a problem, though. In order to receive joy, we have to be open to it. People can and do refuse to be happy. Some people choose to hurt. They spend life licking their wounds, being lonely, living in the past. If they can't have what they want, they refuse to want what they have. If the situation isn't perfect, it isn't acceptable. If they can't have that, they don't want this. They make a long face the hallmark of virtue. They suffer well and they love to suffer.

Openness to joy in the present is a sign of faith, of mental health, of maturity. There is some happiness in the midst of every suffering.

Question:

Think of an unhappy period of your life. What was the happiness in it? What is your greatest burden right now? What is the happiness in it?

_____
_____
_____

DAY 3/*REFLECTION*. Read and respond.

Joy is the infallible sign of the presence of God. (Leon Bloy)

Question:

Do you agree with this statement? Explain. Do you know a joyful person? Who?

DAY 4/*PERSONAL REFLECTION.*

Now write your own insights or problems with this verse as diary or dialogue or testimony or debate. Write with feeling and with honesty.

*Give us joy to balance our affliction,
 for the years when we knew misfortune.*

DAY 5/*MEMORIZE*.

Write from memory the psalm verse you've been contemplating. (Remember the psalm number, too.)

_____
_____
_____
_____
_____

At this point in my life this psalm verse

_____
_____
_____
_____
_____
_____
_____
_____
_____
_____
_____
_____
_____
_____
_____

ACTION.
Think of someone you know who is in a down period of life. Do something nice for them. How did they react?

WEEK 49
DAY 1/*PSALM 92*

O God, how great are your works,
 How deep are your designs...

Say the psalm verse over and over throughout the entire day until it becomes automatic, until it comes without effort, until you've memorized it.

DAY 2/*REFLECTION*.

Say the psalm verse to yourself thoughtfully several times. Now read the reflection and respond to it any way you can.

I learn by going where I have to go," Theodore Roetke wrote. That's an important concept. All of life cannot be planned. openness is its key.

If we let God have our lives, then life is always going our way whether it seems so or not. Life is full of miracles so quiet we cannot see them, so simple we cannot recognize them and, consequently, we often miss them or, worse, we insist on recasting our lives in our own image. We put our hearts into things that we know are less than God. We don't get trapped; we go willingly. We make our own pits of excess, or dependencies, or self-interests. Then we go through life complaining about what we ourselves have done.

We forget that life as it is given to us is good; that life as it has been given is given for our good. We miss the deep design of our own lives.

As the Eastern mystic says: "O wonder: I chop wood; I draw water from the well."

Question:

Name two good things in life that you take for granted, that you never think to be grateful for.

DAY 3/*REFLECTION*. Read and respond.

Great ideas, it has been said,
come into the world
as gently as doves.
Perhaps, then,
if we listen attentively,
we shall hear amid the uproar
of empires and nations
a faint flutter of wings
a gentle stirring of life and hope.
            (Albert Camus)

Question:

Name one great idea — historical or contemporary — that you think fits this description.

DAY 4/*PERSONAL REFLECTION.*

Now write your own insights or problems with this verse as diary or dialogue or testimony or debate. Write with feeling and with honesty.

O God, how great are your works,
 How deep are your designs...

DAY 5/*MEMORIZE.*

Write from memory the psalm verse you've been contemplating. (Remember the psalm number, too.)

At this point in my life this psalm verse

ACTION.
Write a letter to someone from your past — a teacher, a neighbor, a relative — and thank them for something they did for you that you now appreciate in a new way.

WEEK 50

DAY 1/PSALM 84

*They are happy who dwell in your house;
They walk with ever growing strength.*

Say the psalm verse over and over throughout the entire day until it becomes automatic, until it comes without effort, until you've memorized it.

DAY 2/REFLECTION

Say the psalm verse to yourself thoughtfully several times. Now read the reflection and respond to it any way you can.

I can tell if I'm really becoming spiritually stronger by asking myself what I have wrestled with in the spiritual life: with money and things, with relationships, with self-will, with superficiality, with addictions, with indifference, with spiritual dishonesty, with control of time and participation and people, with parochialism, with independence. Has anything changed? It should have. Have I come closer to God or am I still only going through the motions?

The worst thing is to die immersed in self without knowing God and to waste a short life on insignificant things.

Question:

Name at least two issues in life that you have gone through and grown beyond because you realized that they were either unworthy or self-destructive byways.

_____
_____
_____
_____
_____

DAY 3/*REFLECTION*. Read and respond.

The sole meaning of life is to serve humanity. (Leo Tolstoy)

Question:
Finish this sentence: The sole meaning of life is _____

DAY 4/*PERSONAL REFLECTION.*

Now write your own insights or problems with this verse as diary or dialogue or testimony or debate. Write with feeling and with honesty.

*They are happy who dwell in your house;
They walk with ever growing strength.*

DAY 5/*MEMORIZE.*

Write from memory the psalm verse you've been contemplating. (Remember the psalm number, too.)

_____
_____
_____
_____
_____
_____

At this point in my life this psalm verse
_____
_____
_____
_____
_____
_____
_____
_____
_____
_____
_____
_____
_____
_____
_____
_____

ACTION.
Draw a square on this page. Inside it, write an event or issue that you spent more time or emotion on than it deserved. Draw lines through it.

WEEK 51

DAY 1/PSALM 89

How long, O God;
Will you hide yourself forever?

Say the psalm verse over and over throughout the entire day until it becomes automatic, until it comes without effort, until you've memorized it.

DAY 2/REFLECTION.

Say the psalm verse to yourself thoughtfully several times. Now read the reflection and respond to it any way you can.

F aith is not for good times. Faith is for darkness. We have to learn to let things be; not to dwell on apparent losses, even when we don't understand, even when we feel the pain of aloneness and uncertainty.

Question:

What is going on in your life now that leaves you with the pain of not being able to understand?

DAY 3/*REFLECTION*. Read and respond.

A fisherman in China sat fishing with a straight needle, year after year. People wondered and talked about this strange fisherman until the story reached the emperor, who decided to take a look at this phenomenon in person. "Now tell me, my good man," the emperor said, "what do you hope to catch with that straight needle?" And the man answered, "You, your majesty."

Question:

Has God ever "caught you" by fishing with a straight needle? Explain.

DAY 4/*PERSONAL REFLECTION.*

Now write your own insights or problems with this verse as diary or dialogue or testimony or debate. Write with feeling and with honesty.

How long, O God;
   Will you hide yourself forever?

DAY 5/*MEMORIZE.*

Write from memory the psalm verse you've been contemplating. (Remember the psalm number, too.)

_____
_____
_____
_____
_____

At this point in my life this psalm verse

_____
_____
_____
_____
_____
_____
_____
_____
_____
_____
_____
_____
_____
_____

ACTION.
Pick up any two things in your room. What do they have to do with your spiritual life?

WEEK 52
DAY 1/PSALM 119

I am lost like a sheep;
Seek your servant for I remember your commands.

Say the psalm verse over and over throughout the entire day until it becomes automatic, until it comes without effort, until you've memorized it.

DAY 2/REFLECTION.

Say the psalm verse to yourself thoughtfully several times. Now read the reflection and respond to it any way you can.

The psalm brings a very poignant insight with it. The psalmist does not say, "I remember your commands; therefore, I will seek you." No, the psalmist says, "I'm lost; therefore, you seek me."

The truth is that there are times in life when we simply don't seem to have enough energy or will to seek God, even though we have the theological background to "remember the commands" and know that we should. That's when this psalm is so important. It reminds us that when hard times come all we have to do is pray, "I am lost like a sheep; seek your servant for I remember your commands," and then watch for the answer.

We have to remember that commitment is not all feeling. In fact, moments of real commitment are often without feeling at all. The task is to cultivate the spiritual life until it is our deepest happiness and most lasting joy. And then in hard, dry times to simply say over and over: "I am lost like a sheep; seek your servant. . . ."

Question:

When were you "lost like a sheep"? What brought you back?

DAY 3/*REFLECTION*. Read and respond.

Rabbi Barukh's grandson, Yehiel, was once playing hide-and-seek with another boy. He hid himself and waited for his playmate to find him. When he had waited for a long time, he came out of his hiding place, but the other was nowhere to be seen. Now Yehiel realized that his friend had not looked for him from the very beginning. This made him cry, and crying he ran to his grandfather and complained of his faithless friend. Then tears brimmed in Rabbi Barukh's eyes and he said, "God says the same thing: 'I hide but no one wants to seek me.'"
(Tales of the Hasidim)

Question:

Is your God a "hidden God"? What does it mean "to seek God"? Do you seek God? How?

DAY 4/*PERSONAL REFLECTION.*

Now write your own insights or problems with this verse as diary or dialogue or testimony or debate. Write with feeling and with honesty.

I am lost like a sheep;
   Seek your servant for I remember your
      commands.

DAY 5/*MEMORIZE.*

Write from memory the psalm verse you've been contemplating. (Remember the psalm number, too.)

At this point in my life this psalm verse

ACTION.
Play a tape or record of spiritual music. Listen to the words carefully.